BOOKS BY MARY KINZIE

AUTUMN EROS   1991

SUMMERS OF VIETNAM (*including* MASKED WOMEN)   1990

THE THRESHOLD OF THE YEAR   1982

Autumn Eros

& Other Poems

Mary Kinzie

Autumn Eros

& Other Poems

Alfred A. Knopf   New York
1991

THIS IS A BORZOI BOOK
PUBLISHED BY ALFRED A. KNOPF, INC.

Grateful acknowledgment is made to the following publications in which certain poems were originally published:

AGNI REVIEW: Waltzing Matilda
AMERICAN POETRY REVIEW: Strawberry Pipe
THE NEW YORKER: Lunar Frost
SALMAGUNDI: Pine; Little Brown Jug; The Other Children; Summer Globe (in an earlier version); Sun and Moon; Dweller in the Forest; Mannikin; L'Estate; Faith
SHENANDOAH: The Current; Drawing Through Fever
SOUTHWEST REVIEW: Sparrows; Palazzo; Circadian
STANFORD HUMANITIES REVIEW: This Phoebe
THREEPENNY REVIEW: Learning the World; Boy
TRIQUARTERLY: Sound Waves; Autumn Eros
YALE REVIEW: Canicula

I am grateful to the John Simon Guggenheim Memorial Foundation for a fellowship that enabled me to compose a number of these poems, and to the President's Fund for the Humanities at Northwestern University for a research grant during completion of the manuscript.

I would also like to thank Leslie Scalapino and the Poetry Society of America for awarding "L'Estate" the 1988 Celia B. Wagner Prize. Thanks as well to TriQuarterly and the Illinois Arts Council for the poetry prize awarded to "Autumn Eros."

Finally, a word to those invaluable friends who have sustained me: I am in your debt. M.K.

Library of Congress Cataloging-in-Publication Data

Kinzie, Mary.
    Autumn eros and other poems / by Mary Kinzie. — 1st ed.
        p. cm.
    ISBN 0-394-58992-0
    1. Mothers and daughters—Poetry. I. Title.
PS3561.I59A97   1991
811'.54—dc20   91-52718
                                                     CIP

Manufactured in the United States of America
First Edition

FOR MY PARENTS
AND THEIR OTHER CHILDREN,
MY BROTHERS,
RICHARD HUEY KINZIE AND HARRY ERNST KINZIE III,
AND MY SISTER, MABLE BARBIE KINZIE

AND FOR PHOEBE

CONTENTS

LUNAR FROST

L'ESTATE

Contents

AUTUMN EROS

Lunar Frost

Surely, whispers in the glassy corridor
Never trouble their dream.
Never, for them, the dark turreted house reflects itself
In the depthless stream.

HAPPY FIELDS

Adam in paradise when he was asked
To look into Dante's mind and speak the wish
Unnamed yet, but as clear as Adam was
Himself beneath the veil of flame,
Rippling his limbs
In a joyful premonition
Of response so bone and shoulder
Streamed against the sack,
                              at once knew
How, skein over skein, by a thread
He would unravel his array
Of memories from the quickened past . . .

    The six brief hours in Eden;
    Following these,
    His body's thousand years
    Parching under the tree,
    Life grown dimmer than the earth
    Was hard;
            then forty centuries
    Of stasis after death, waiting
    For Christ to tip the cup
    Of waiting, everything now
    Clear as a glass—even Eve
    (But never the least residue
    Of hatred); and ever,
    Floating out of time,
    Those lovely Hebrew names
    He had given to the beasts . . .

Truths of a freshness he could feel
The shuttle of language
Rush across, and fix
In order fast
Like fabric looming

Till, eager beneath the living sleeve
Of speech about him growing,
He moved in pleasure—
And slow the living man
Thought out his mortal,
Callow questions (to Adam
Dearer than children)
About archaic life:

    To have the answer,
    To be called on,
    Was very heaven.

TEXAS, WITH DRY MIMOSA

The darkness should be cool, but it is not.
Tufts of Bermuda grass seem also hot,
Slowly taking hold in the white ground,
Gritty and resistant. There is the sound
Of water running down excelsior
In the neighbors' air conditioner.
We are trying to save, still have a fan,
And will not sleep much now, do what we can.
The sandbox starts to sift with restless things.
I move my chair off.
                    I hear arguings
As they are put to bed—the younger ones.
I was a believer like them once.
Bathed in the light. That is how we begin.
Washing in God as if to wash Him in;
Praying the Mary beads that we would keep
Under the pillow, whispering through our sleep
Till we could lean our whole weight on one deep
Swell of unthinking.

                    That was earlier.
Now, not only is the starlight far,
We see the stars because they are burning up,
Or were when their light started to come low.
Perhaps they are burnt up now, from long ago?
A wind is coming. The mimosa's bent
And shakes from feathery blooms a citron scent,

And sand is drinking from my sister's cup.

PINE

To the next in line

Aisles of Southern evergreens exhale
Their dusty-sharp and cold piney aromas
Somewhat conflicting according to their species
And their nearness to the road or water.
Growing so straight and in such multitudes
They look like the girders of some installation
Abandoned halfway-through to the kelp and coral
Of earth: To branches flocked with green and laden
With little lives rippling the frame like a vine
Suffused with color, whose intricate song like a flail
Sweeps far, then near, is taken up by others,
Then, with the delaying of a bell,
Shudders in the limits of its silence
Before descending in a flood of notes.

So the forest undulates, each formal fir
Bestowing with the sleeve of its kimono
Gestures of benediction, unmistaken
But, above my head, remote, absorbed
In their own conversation, like my parents
Whose distraction, stylized into touch,
Liberates that thing in me that needs
To be anonymous. All children have it,
Even recognize it in each other,
Like kits of sister foxes, and keep clear.

Watching what I think is the natural world
Where it overlaps with us, out on a picnic,
Someone who is more an interruption
Of impression than the thing itself,
Someone so close to me as to be neuter,
Colorless and slight as an old May fly,
Drifts across the sandy needle-heaped trail.
I take him in by narrowing my eyes,
Each movement lizard-like and gradual;

6

Hypnotized into a huge acceptance,
It seems to me I might, in time, still suffer
The myriad lives to sniff me out in safety,
Even rest upon me and doze off—
The child who shudders at a moth translated
Into one who might affect their kinship.
Do the pines bring out this abstract bravery—
Their towering gloom and sameness, yet their freshness?—
It is like staring with the vision locked on nothing,
Except that the whole body grows myopic,
Focused on that near infinity
Amassed diffusely at the tingling senses.

Sleepwalking through the knowledge of my absence
From the dinner blanket (although it is not late),
And sensing the place I am not as a waste
Unruly spout of grit and wind, I drag
With a fine reluctance through the standing trunks
Toward the voices that outline the soughing
Until they are small words, and not mere nature:
At once, they seem on the verge of my own name
Until the place is filled with piquancy.
But there, a few yards distant, goes the boy
In his familiar clothes and sad demeanor
Looking for his whistle, face screwed up,
Unaware of me in his sweet anguish,
Sand on his knees and one cheek, each hair wrong,
Arms lashing aimlessly then hanging stiff
As, in a soundless fury, his mouth says,
Yow yow.
      Whether spurred on by discontent
On this grand scale or (deeper therapy)
Swept under any memory of pain,
He concentrates again on his desire,
Condensing in his fists a force of will
So clear to see as the fierce thoughts take shape

I feel almost aggrieved he does not see me . . .
But, zealous, his eyes dilate on a plan
As he trots back out to the angry beach.

Unmagicked, flat, excluded from his wishes,
I wish we had more than the air in common,
That, in our disconnection, we adhered.
In an old photograph, I take his hand
In which he holds an egg to scrutinize.
I look up, quirky and exasperated,
Like a wife whose husband has a hobby
She never liked, but (sort of) understands.
Like her, I loved him once, we had our secrets,
Which now seem to be scattered in this wood.

I am a mere few shaggy trees inside it,
Can glimpse the dark pines on the other shore.
A cold low slash of stark blue water yawns
Open below the buttery bowl of space
In open sunshine. On the beach, the clusters
Of families far down the sand, the wisps
Rising from their votive fires, our blanket
Tended by an aunt, the adults gone
Somewhere on the water with those children
Nearer to hand (do they assume that I
Have drifted harmlessly toward my own ship?)—
It is a scene of bits, of desolation.
Because I had abandoned them in mind,
I am convinced they never will come back.
My aunt, who died last year, tries to console me.

LITTLE BROWN JUG

He jigs the little baby on his knee.
She crows as he sings almost tenderly
The bouncing tune about the happy pair
Who loved her—with her brown eyes and brown hair
The very incandescences of brown.

She does not want for him to put her down.
However tired he is, he is happy so,
Holding the round child who won't let him go
While Mother gets our dinner and I lay
The many places and Daddy sings away
The song I do not know refers to him
Years after this, and what he would become.

Yet when I saw him playing with her there,
The little sister I loved, too, her hair
And eyes so shining, I thought *she*
Was the sweet drink he craved: "Don't I love thee?"

ROSARY

O Mary, we crown thee with blossoms today,
Queen of the angels, Queen of the May.

The dream showed how the kitchen gardens throve
Along new miles of glinting fence. Like an enchanted moth
I traced but did not touch the smooth unbroken rinds
And huge planetary globes of gourd and of tomato.
Even the petals of the tall still zinnias
Stood out individual orange, rose, and blood
Beside the simple stoops, three sideless stairs of formed
Cement, some giving off the chalky smell of paving
Recently sprinkled. Then arose the neighboring smell
Of masonry, dry-sour like bread, baked earth, or fur
Or feathers or like the arrowhead of cuttlebone
In the cage on one empty porch, a chartreuse parakeet's
With nostrils set in blue. The bird addressed my shadow
With a rough discursive warble, voice-like, brotherly,
And I felt it with my one hand perching on my other,
Its bone-frame tiny and its confidential heart
Beating much faster than my own heart could ever beat.

Mild and small, at length the little parrot's body
Became unbearable to hold, as if it were
Explosive. As I urged it through its gate, I was moved,
Torn to the blond stony ground in a night that was suddenly much
Hotter and larger than before, filled with stars
Visible only because they were burning violently
And fear became the emblem of my truth: that I
Had been brought back to this forbidding place to try
Again to dry my will (although my flesh shook, thirsty);
Then a hard frightful *slapping* sounded behind and above me.

There were the mother and other children kneeling down
Saying the rosary at one of the beds. An attic fan
Labored to draw the blistering air across their shoulders.

The beads fell forward through their fingers in
The drone of the "Hail, Mary," mechanical by now,
A hollow sentenceless terrain of beads of sound,
Combed hives of consonants and vowels in the new
Hot treeless house with a screened-in porch along the side
Where the parakeet could leave its cage, and no breeze came,
One of the boys always asleep by the end.

                                       One block
Away the helicopters tore through the night to land,
Ominous despite their tired civilian cargo,
Flailing across the roof in anger at our prayers—
Engines that deliberately repressed our words
Or roughly lifted us a few beats out of sleep,
Warning us that this world, too, would have to end.

Through my sleep these rancorous dark engines swept,
Flying closer, more of them, and more vigilant,
In persistent Armageddon of the remnant evil.
There were no more good men. The bomb had found them first
Out in the sun with nothing but their skin for armor.
I was at school; then I am running to reach home
But the night flares up in charred horizons and gas fires,
Heat that whips the rubble and the carapaces
Of the choppers glinting everywhere on earth
Like flies on meat. Our crown of blossoms for the Queen
Of the May, our little melodies for Mother Mary
Are mocked to ashes by the metallic apparitions
Slapping the heated oily air into a whirlwind
That slides down as I touch where our house was, then leaps,
Lying on its side like a top to nip at me .

*   *   *

I have awakened, torn from sleep, and face the fierce
Moon that makes the yellow ground go white, the sky
Phosphorescent and marine.

Rosary

                              With relief, I hear
The old black fan oscillating on a stool
At the foot of the bed. Its blades, ordinarily brown,
When they whirred were golden, adding to my relief
That this was the world, the rosary heaped under the pillow,
And that *she* was there, small frame, warm skin, a different pulse,
The sister of two or three who was the core of my heart
When I thought about her, and when I did not,
The faintly smiling sill of my life, like a far door
Into an idle future hung pleasantly ajar.

BOY

*I thought at first he never would
start talking. Then when he started,
I thought he would never stop.*

By day his world extends, far, knotted, hot.
Wasps long as fingers drag their jet black legs.
The concrete of the steps is cool but not
Cooling as a fine grit sticks to his legs.
How much he knows of them, no one suspects.
Mother is bathing. He is in her room,
Picks up a bottle filled with red perfume,

Red as his hair. The bottle like a spire
Thrusts toward a point of crystalline desire
Scattering rainbows on the mirror higher
Than he can touch. He does not try. Wire
Hangers whisper, curtains clasp the fire
The sun starts to pour downward on this side,
Which means a nap with his eyes open wide

And a hot fretfulness that is like fear
Brushing at the faint temples of his head.
The others are at school, but will appear
In strange unravelings of joy like thread,
Also mixed with dread.
Crossing the street in danger, down the block,
They will lift the shield of their majestic talk.

His mother comes out. She has put her robe
Around the baby she wears in her skin.
He may not climb against that living globe;
But with her cool arms she still draws him in
As if he were her boy, had always been.
They look among her bracelets for a toy
That might be helpful to a napping boy.

Inevitably, nothing is enough
To make up for her absence. The family rob
Him hourly of themselves until, weak, gruff,
He throws his hand out with a practice sob,
The bracelet bouncing with a hollow throb—
Sounds that mingle like an overture
To blackness, solitude, and forfeiture.

He nearly suffocates in his defense.
He cannot get the whole out that he knows.
When he jumps to be free, there is the fence
Of his quick temper and his dirty clothes
And the ill-fated moment that he chose
To climb into the lap and claim that kiss.
His tantrum then just sets their prejudice.

Curious and fragile he slips through
The pattern of their futures like a ghost.
Unlike his actions, his door is not closed
So he can drift into his sister's room
When he can't sleep at night. What comforts most
Is being too good, waiting, as in play,
Then climbing up when she says that he may.

THE OTHER CHILDREN

We are in the car and going south.
At the tired tip of Missouri, the weather lifts.
Books did not tell me this—this sky, this sea—
Would be so: the mouth of the Orinoco?—
Where the sun was reddening its mouth?—
Or the islands, upside down, to which we rose
Like minnows in the jar
Curious for food.
In our water bubble, my smaller brother
Sleepily less cross, my tiny sister drooling on her dress—
How could I fail one instant in my love
For these near worlds, breathing minutiae,
Damp globes of cloud and gaiety and will?

There, I tell them, trying a phrase I had read,
Are the Islands of the West
With no snow and apples of copper.
Pointing to the purple tracts of sky
Blazed round by yellow,
I asked the other children, *Could they see*
The Islands of the Blest (this was correct)
Where you never get mad and you never need rest?—
Though they are drifting from me
Into that water
Where there is neither anger nor memory
And where, reserved, perfected,
They are less real (diminishing in sleep,
More dear), while briefly beside me glows
From each shape on the seat
A squib of formless interest.

LUNAR FROST

For my father

The night of the day
That broke up at sunset in a beadwork
Of islands, my head
On the hot window glass, which gave
Back to me over the highway a face on an angle,
Tinted green over white like a lily
Or angel leaning down against the car—
It was then night drew apart
Like a planet the frost had raked level,
Cold, scored, abandoned.

                    Ghastly,
The stars as we drove
Chattered with fear from their stations
Far above, unable
To warm us, or each other.

Night journey. The only warmth, from the dashboard
Far ahead where the announcer
Talks low with my father. They say
Nothing that I can hear. In the dark, my mother
Quiet beside him with the youngest,
My father has told me to sleep
So he can take his comfort from
The warm controls, hearing a neutral voice.
I am for him another sleepy child
Whom he can see, but doesn't, in his mirror,
Awake alone.

          Yet I have done
What he said to, been kind, been of use,
Learned to iron, and save.
And thought. He has told me to think.
So, when the lesson strums forward at school
With a dull breath like telephone poles going by,

16

I try to expand till my mind fills my body,
Even my ankles, even my eyes;
And as I fill with more than I can know—
The thought of number and the abstract term,
Collective noun, the beings that were once—
I start to shrink down to the facts,
I tear back all I know till I don't know it,
And I can see the jagged
Flicker at the core
Prior to understanding,
Tearing thought down into pieces
That sit about oddly under a different light,
Strange, hard, anonymous.

                 I question
Everything, break the world down
By questions again
Into incompletion, as it was
In the beginning:

Why isn't shadow
Beside you, your size,
Not loose as a stain
That sinks over what's in the way
(These clots of weed and stuttering
Of rock along the highway)? Does the soul
Of someone who is falling out of life
Fall among such things?

                 Will water
In the desert also stagger
In the light that mimics it, until,
Risen from the shelf of thirst
Like Indians wavering in a last gauze
Of sunstroke, the fainting rivulets
Boil off to sand?

What is the sin for which
These lifeless places are the punishment?—
Laziness? impatience?—when one sinks
Into sleep in the garden (where Christ
Watches the hour)? What is it seeps
Away in the disciple's heart?

Would it be sin to eat His fish
(Even *His*), once you see how they are
Hauled in, hooked—all the quick
Darters, sunfish, bass, rainbow—
Through their rough inhuman mail
And hollow stare?

                    And then,
Huddled together at the final hour
As we are here, eyes on the dark
Where all the warmth dissolves
And every shape is hooded,
When would the narrow soldiers
Realize they will not leave
The garrison? that Santa Anna
Must lay his curving sabre
Even into the living chamber
Of the breast? Does the mind widen
With a wail
For the cold through-coursing
Of the gouts of dying?

With these last words,
Hooked at the end by my question,
I open to my fear. It is here,
Trying to outrun routine in the ever
Fainter countries of the lesson,
That I stumble into my smoky blank,
My center: Knowing of dying

A thought I see ahead with a rough
Porous rind like a column, abraded and hollow,
That can't even stand in its shadow,
All thinking broken, then worn down to this:
Do you know when you're dying?
When you lie, one night in the cold,
Does the ceiling glide open, like an eye
Into whose emptiness you start to fall
(Though you fall up)? Are you extinguished
Like a fleck of burning paper
Sucked out the chimney
Into a broad lake of cold, where there is
No more fire and the fish
Move endlessly away on all sides?

Here is no fire.
Here is a wound
Made in me by the smiling metal
Which as I think about it
Starts to pour.

        In the distance
My father cannot find another station
(I think, the radio, he means gasoline).
We slow through a dead town, the motor breathing;
Pull into unmanned places bathed in neon
That purples our mouths
And turns the rusted drums and glass moon-green.
Mother turns to me her brown eyes
And loosened kerchief, but her longed-for nearness
Comes like a sharpened stone:
She will die before me;
There is a moment, to come,
When a worse solitude than this
Would drift across the acres
Where Mother, Father will be forced in fact

To disappear, and I to sink into
Mere sleep, though I tremble, weep,
And watch the rigid hour
Like an iron lung
Press shining, around me, their deaths,
Which I will see, where I lie frozen,
In the sparkling rearview mirror above my head.

SPARROWS

For my sister

Night's fallen. I wait at a light.
Two girls go forward in slow rain;
Brown clothes, sweet faces in the lamp
Show up, their hair a little damp,
Coats similarly belted and
The younger takes the elder's hand,
Then, to judge from her light gauzy mane,
She shivers with delight.

The traffic gathers. Engines race.
Above the din, I hear them chat
About some happiness: Someday
To spread their hair and fly away?—
It seemed they had. The younger's wing
Was stroked to stop her shivering,
Which, as they flew, subsided into grace.
Shifting gears, I envied that.

ELD

The scene, a place I know, rather unpleasant
And scarcely nature, the sense of anguish crescent;

If not yet dying's canyon, yet the shape
Of old tautology begins to gape

Across time's desert: What I have to spare,
It wastes. No more for ever any share

In floating being—even family
Tepid from familiarity

Till I can see them catching on my fears
From which their eyes encourage mine to tears.

Something was wanted here, amid the trash
Of nightmare and remorse's moaning lash,

Doom furtive like an adumbrated cat
Among the ill-joined props of habitat;

In code, that taunt of apathetic bliss
Still in the bud, yet slick as muscle is,

Among the heaps of matter and rough wall
In air through which I feel the cosmos fall.

Even here, or is it *just* here that I think
I spy a passageway like thirst, like drink?—

Something the mind cannot yet form along,
Tasting of several senses, headed wrong

But plunging (with a shiver) to the end
Where time is blind and mind and body blend

In an old faith, uncanny to its core
Rooted in doubt, that one must give up more

Than one had ever gathered in before
Real life would stretch beyond the still-fast door.

Every sect required the cell's restraint
Before the bolt was loosened into saint.

Even war insisted on this story,
Stories themselves did, creeds, *a fortiori*

That our rewards came in proportion to
The practice crippling us as we broke through,

Boring us, too, as hell's routine would glaze
The dancers moving through one stagnant phase

Where bodies sob. Peculiarly akin
Such virtue was, in payment, to a sin.

Stalled in this foreground limbo of the soul,
Too far to miss how shy I fell the goal,

I saw I could not win—renounce, sit still,
Sleep to the world, above all, break the will

And make it feel easy. Well begun
Came to sound worse than never having done.

Was it a sex thing? To start growing dull
In face of force so random-volatile?

Where was its source? beyond? And yet I saw
Figures amassing like automata

Of inner light, commanding that I *try*:
Say over the worn words until they cry,

Weird with release, as when the ward unlocks
To the flat charm provided by the fox . . .

I could not say them over consciously.
The world of repetition closed to me

Where drop and crumb are numbered, where the tree
Bends to its load of sameness joyfully,

Where through a life of loose beatitude
In which my single study was the good

(So that I accidentally acquired
Stepmother, steward, steed, a spouse, a tired

Yeoman who drank wine till his loins hurt,
Wild birds to pick the lentils from the dirt

Where they again were scattered by the crone
Whose heart was ashen and whose blood was stone,

A huntsman to dispatch the evil cook
Who cut my head off and enchained the brook),

They would reward me that I was exempt
From rage at being mocked, forlorn, unkempt.

And yet this world of bloodshed, hate, ablution
Answered to some finer restitution

As, to things, their film of sparkling fear
That coats the drugged castle year by year,

Buried in peat and pelt and sift of grime
In symbols shimmering backward into time

But even at the limit of the trope
Outlined with a sober band of hope:

> *Haloed in swans, an act that raises tears,*
> *The little princess dumb for seven years*
>
> *Until they recompense her sacrifice*
> *In ringing speech. Others get back their eyes;*
>
> *Some necks; some elbows. All the maimed are healed.*
> *The miller's girl, whose goodness was no shield—*
>
> *Because she had no hands to eat the pear,*
> *The king sent to have made a silver pair;*
>
> *Until (ensues here much vicissitude)*
> *Her hands grew back, so she could eat her food.*

In all these tales the children, orphaned, grave
In rejection, hungry, lost, behave

As if initiated to some rite
That took their blind adherence to come right.

None of them seemed to question why the sea
Of rubble must be ordered or the tree

Brought down with a handsaw made of glass
(It broke at once) or why the dress must pass

Through a needle's eye without once raking
The metal edge although one's heart was breaking.

And it was this prevented me from praying,
Locked me out of all reach of obeying—

Not just too weak, too stubborn. I foreknew
That what would waste my time, I could not do,

Even when this forced me to stand by
Observing the last sibling, warm, dumb, shy,

Through the mirror's sooty verdigris
Stumble into the very lap of bliss,

Performing the old actions, brief, banal,
With a temper that was beatifical,

The sieve or scissors or the crystal axe
So gently handled that the nails relax,

The water mounts up, and the heavy shears
Cut pretty shapes in what swords could not pierce.

The business of the soul is done by these
Third sons, last daughters, fools who tend the geese,

Those one might have been (but that the thorn
Had worked into the heart and turned to scorn).

One sees in them the child one, just now, was,
Fading with a solemn animus

Or sheer incomprehension staring through
Us as the smaller creatures do,

From whom one's being, offered no resistance,
Poured out, at length, to this increasing distance

Across all that waste time open to youth
When the days breathed, and the green, smooth

Skin of warm nature stretched without a flaw
From a center out of reach—like a camera,

Whose shutter curves in on a shining eye,
Or shimmering in memory like a dragonfly

Dark in its bulk, veined by the trembling gauze
That fans its film across the body's laws.

At the heart of every garden hummed that clue:
The thing that rustled almost out of view

Smelling of clover hidden by a yew;
Or a little water trickling muddy-blue

From around a rock; a locust screaming up
The scale, then going still; a buttercup,

Wilted; the roses lavishing their scent
On a prone collie on the house intent

Who looks right through the thicket, her long tongue
Banked by the lines of teeth and overhung

By yielding folds of muzzle. *O soft creature,*
Look at me, I breathed, *become my teacher,*

Transform through feeling and draw off this pain
Foolish as summer, heavy as hot rain——

But the dog trotted off into the past
Where I, inert from grief, lost her at last.

Would she have answered that eternity
Had been lodged in my mind lest I should see

What had been done in seven days—how he
Had done it?—down to knitting me

Into the womb until I should draw breath
And start to form another rune of death?

Or did this knowledge only come to those
Who see the warrant with such knowledge close?

What was the cosmos but a shiftless ebb
Of tinkering to cover up thin web?

And in the loose space, which poured in from afar
Like something rising in me, my life's star

Haled the last daylight toward it; elegiac
Wept, then hardened, in the well of black.

SUMMER GLOBE

Did we go to the water as a charm,
Hoping that aimless sand and waves like razors
Scraping along the blue-black hide of water
Would cure us of our difference? teach us pleasure?

Tricky to ride, sometimes one set us down
For the next to slap the breath out of, and the next.
Fish stank in the air, and decomposing eelgrass,
While out on the rough bruising water clanged
A buoy mad as a kettle left to boil
But pitched like the lowest bell at Requiem.

Far up the shore, the building of gray stucco
Where for a dime you could take off your clothes
And store them—odd vestigial manners
From the East (we always rode home wet:
Water still seemed to us a miracle,
In the desert it wicked away like wind).
On the ground floor, like an installation
To support Athena Polias
In her huge temple, the expectant base
—A waterfountain—raised its shallow dish
Nubby and flecked with local sand suspended
Like frozen atoms in its vast cement,
Images of interstellar pools
Suspended in an interstellar thirst
(Though I doubt the Greeks did much on their hill with water,
Its movements were not what they came to worship).
Two spigots cast up arcs of warmish bubbles
Roping against your mouth, tasting of tin,
While the twin streams raced away in flattening sheets
That striped the basin with a wash of silver
And made a gargling noise deep in the drain.

And as you stood on the chilly bath house floor
Waiting in line, you heard, from everywhere,

A shrieking of children who streamed upon the stairs
Like a natural fluid—even the pale green doors
(Why should this detail unnerve me now?
For the doors and walls of the stalls were made of wood
Mottled with layer on layer of pale
Mint-green paint, which took the fingerprints,
Black-runneled and exact, of every hand)—
Even the wood shut with an oceanic clangor
As in the children's small quick hands like banners
Towels and brightly colored gear would flicker,
On torsos, around their necks . . . Their forms appeared
To soar and flutter like creatures in an aviary
Ominously reversed:
                    You stood inside it,
Caged, picked over, mingled with these strangers,
Doomed to an echoing din of which no word
Was comprehensible and from which flowed
No warmth of friendly recognition.
The buoy marker's bell rang mournfully,
Sealing the cold trap closed with an old cadence,
Alternating light and heavy knowledge,
Bittersweet and low, globe-*globe*, globe-*globe*.

STRAWBERRY PIPE

For my mother

At daybreak I lift to my lips the gift of her cup
(Small and old, but not like flesh). The rim has
A burned gold border like a weeping comet.
Painted on the saucer, and the curve of transparent
China to the left of the scroll-hooked handle,
Designs of red berries hanging from dark stems
As we hung from our parents by a wish
That was their desire—
                                        as we hung from their hands
When we were buckling forward to the pavement
Until we balanced, and then fell like fruit.
(Even before I could summon up this knowledge,
I *knew* I was what my parents always wanted.)

Like shoots in the wet after a hard winter,
There rise up, straggly as fur, gap-toothed as dill,
These fern sprays that seem to tremble behind the leaves,
Dark green, black-veined, of the strawberry vines.
White flowers that will harbinger more berries
Appear in paint beside what they become,
Like parents in all our photographs before us,
Which we confuse with those with us in them,
Except that, then, it's they were the fragrant and pendulous
Like tapestry rosehips, open pistachios,
Like pebbles falling on a hot day to the bottom,
And we, the dry-lipped paperwhites of spring.
Now we are the purple-with-life. We hang. We pull down.
We burst with the hot contours of our sinking
While they elude our gravity, whisked
By weariness from our orbit, weightless, sleepy,
Pale with use and willing to be scentless
As cool white poppies on a cup and plate.

Of the three cursive signatures (saucer,
Cup-front, cup-back), all meant to say "Strawberry Ripe,"

31

The one I face when I drink is worn to "Pipe"
As though this were the grove where they had played
In the past, listening to my pipings.
Across the water, one can hear their voices
(Even if the air were empty now).
The water is leaf-green, the sky late blue,
And Mother is swimming far out to the float.
In the lisping shallow brown lake water
Beside me, relatives—my uncles, her brothers
Jack and Claude and Chalmers and Robert—would whistle,
"My, your mother is a lovely swimmer,"
Making their very sighs sound like the South,
And they and I would look at her together.
Her long arms stroked along her bathing cap
Like a breath of surf, like the lapping of wings
Against a constant horizon as she grew smaller,
More alarming, petal-white, more like a tiny bird
Beating with my heartbeat: *Mother, mother.*

Bathing suit bright yellow. Legs and arms
Tawny. Crisp brown hair. She waves at me.
She is standing up, a life-sized human.
It is a hot late Carolina afternoon.
That is my lovely mother on the float.
And I have chiggers, and don't know how to swim.

Memory. You Fooler. You Unfair.
Fruit of the unforgotten twisted past
At once sweet to swooning, and alive with stings.
Last summer, we could hardly pick our apples;
Clouds of danger rose from the ground at each step.
I found one Golden Delicious by Arcimboldo
With white-striped bomber-hornets instead of meat.
The peeling I plucked it by fell away like a tarp,
And in my palm clung a swarm of tiny apples
Feasting on the memory of cider,

Till, one by one, they shot off as if bit,
And to my terror left nothing to hurl down.

So with the truth, so laughter, harm, and passion—
All throb in the hollow, recollected, dark, and
Artificial chamber of the self
Feeding on each other's borrowed juice,
Coherent out of habit and long standing,
Scattered at the footfall of the flesh.
So with my mother's beauty—nose, nail, and thigh,
Molecules compounded differently
Than the bronze work from the past—now small and old
(But not like flesh), she moves through all my being
Piercing me with her smile, shell of the future
In which I fit, into which I shall grow.

And so with love as well. Cleaving the water,
Graceful, but never as wholly self-given
To one moment as she seemed to be,
I swim in the indoor pool at the Church Street "Y"
Two days a week. Rapture of the deep
Comes on me, sometimes, after one-half mile
When someone swims alongside under me—
My shadow, who is male; or a huge mammal
Whose unweaned, slippery child I am. I play.
I do a dolphin-quiver with my trunk,
Maintaining the forward arm-over-arm of the crawl,
No let-up on the flutter of my kick
(The very monotony of this makes me gay),
Until, giddy with time to come and hope to have,
Arm over arm insistently as longing,
I cup with my palm my throbbing husband's neck
And pull him to my lips, remembering
Sun raying through water; caromed back from shore,
The laughter of my mother as something from under
Pulled at her ankle (Daddy): "You fooler! Unfair!"

A visor of tears sweeps down from my bathing cap
As I push off from under for another lap.
How odd, I think, that the happy are damned
With the wicked to suffer the same: Blurred force,
The weakening of the integument
By which are worked both muscle and idea
Beginning with the little we remember
Dimming into typographic error,
Pun, empty peeling, echo, water, night.

L'Estate

And yellow hair is poured along the ground
From the bent neck of time.

THE DAY ROPE

The counselors grow angry with their lot, looking at one another
Over the heads of the little ones, in the wet rising heat,
At the unaltering earliness of the morning: So much left
Of time before they could collapse into the great evening quarrels
More deeply tested than the unfledged mistrust of their companions
That shrinks against the light.
                              The two most shapeless ones spread out
On the only shaded bench and whisper furtively but knowing
As if to be overheard by all the mothers cooing to their young,
—All those soft creatures combing over what life offered them—
Rising occasionally to scream fullblooded at the addled children
In their charge guilty only of a kind of drifting from the group,
It was hardly serious, their hearts yet unawakened by revolt, else
Despite the pallor and the extreme ungainliness it seemed the women
Had consigned them to—too gross, or too thin, clothes all hung wrong,
At four and five already formed in the gait and bearing of a lifetime—
They could have sniffed the air, bolted, and been blocks away by now.

But when their hour of unwholesome sunlight was deemed complete,
Three whistles summoned the children to assemble down three ropes
Tied to the bodies of the women. They eddied to their places,
Applying to the stem singly at intervals, like leaves,
At which point something in the rigor of the tangle
That roped together their small separations along the infinite
Day reached the fevered head and great gut of the whole,
And the strings of children wavered off toward what sadder,
More inattentive darkness where, while they slept,
Women, turned implacable by all they lacked in the face of youth,
Shamed even by each other's weariness, came and went,
Moving over the hive, checking the combs for the minim of life.

PALAZZO

How quick we are, we take up
Our travels, blithe despite
The spice, the sulfurous
Carbonation, the tittering
Beggars. We do business,
Sit up long, almost healed
And cool as talc.

In the palace floored with marble
Of a rose that tints the air,
We lose each other—we flee apart
Like stars. He takes the salon
Reached by walking through room after room:
How like Polaris! His doors thrown back . . .
The doors to the sky thrown back
In a deliberate show of solitude
Like an open altar's.
                    Hung
At the center of his mind
Like a luminous host,
He relishes the lights along the aisle
Ritually silenced for the afternoon.

Outcropping timidly, the willies
Strum in all the corners
(Our daughter eyes them, too).
He takes personally these
Jitterings in shadow
As if the runes to which his *ratio*
Once was enslaved
Had come back nonsense.

He wants to talk. No. He wishes I would.
Different. Like a *woman*. Tidal
As I quelled his hunger,

His haunting, then sweeping up each stray glance
To my heart like crumbs of pollen the color
Of curry fallen out from the
Beautifully perishing tulip.

Our baby chirping in many languages, the day
Turns up its international volume:
Refracted as if by an ocean, the ruddy
Glazing on the roof-tiles will
Leap, soon, with flame, flush the faces
Adoringly turned toward life,
Long oriental wasps
The while dragging
Against nectar-bearing thickets
Of bloom smoky abdominal sacs.

SUN AND MOON

Complements. Like figures in statuary
Gardens, his a cabled athletic pose, hers
A mermaid's slithering beyond the pool's lip,
    They employ difference

To define, play out such exaggerations
As *Water Floods Rock*. Each the other's private
Lightness tries to ground, or black weight help lighten,
    Acting the obverse.

Struggling to take shape, he contrives a drama
(*Rock Displacing Water*) of will, his *Too-Calm*
Brought to simmering by her permitted *Fire*.
    Fighting indifference,

Meticulous his study, its blazing page
Neat and thoughtful. Hers a rough centrifuge of
Clutter thrown out from the abject crescent where,
    Leaning on elbows,

Head in hand, she worries about his future
While he suffers old indignation. Thus they
Stiffen into orbit, for all their future
    Equal in exile.

What can have put them on this track where turning
Off is met by turning toward exactly?
Instability, which could not have fused them
    But at a distance?

Much more likely sentiment—hall umbrellas
Touching with a hesitant air, their questions
Nervous, soft and forced—even their deference
    Coarsened by sadness

And remorse. The flesh at this hint more shrouded
Glimpses down the vista of itself stiff arms
Like tree limbs in rites so redundant they are
    Thought to lack magic.

Lurid as if scarred by a fire, their garden
Shines with punishment, while the simple planets
Crank about the sky manifesting signs of
    Knowledge and justice.

ENNUI MUNICIPAL

On a baked parkway, trod and uniform,
Sweet-eyed, but listless since the great alarm
That crept up in small inchings to their harm
More slowly than our knowledge that it *was* harm,
The quick wrens watch me, and the curious singers.
There was no flash. This was the blow that lingers.
I roll rough bits of leaves between my fingers.

Autumn is far along despite how warm
It makes one, wandering the wide glare
Diffused across the suburbs with an air
Grinning and agitated. The yards are bare.
The city's nearness presses busily,
Coating with dust, then prying up, the tree,
Then fanning its empty palms:
                                            Could I not see
It had no motive for nor part in this
—This shrinking of the old garden, washed in piss
Then shaken till life loosened in its jaw?
Boiled and paved against bacteria
The town had razed for *me* this replica
Of pond and thicket cleaner and more smooth
Than the pocked orchard and uncouth
Back-up of algae (where the tadpoles bred
Till nature grew a thriving, crawling ooze).
Behold! recycled water from its watershed
Pumped up aloft to spread its diamonded
Regalia in air untenanted
By lowlife!
                        And if it should seem tinged with *red?*—
The air in which the fluoridated fountain
Shatters, while the van of our largesse
Rumbles the pavements, revving pitiless
For our own good—for commerce—braking, too,
As if to test its stop-time for consumers

But in the doing, sickening the redwood
Till it thunders: draining the rich well
Until the very ground gives, then gives out?—
Should we think what in hell?

The salesman even watches for a spell
Though nausea awakens him as well
As the taproot of our future trembles out
—All one might have done if opened out—
The husks of helpful creatures clinging still,
Sarcophagi of their aerating skill.

Their loss leaves more than more work for the few:
Small creatures and small kindnesses abandoned,
The less grow great on less, sick on the well,
And as a town with only space to sell
Will sell down-looking on its citadel,
The virulent in vacancy excel.

*   *   *

Elegiac looms the jazz-bright blue
Dome, dust-gilded, whining like a bell
High pitched but devilish. Devilish the sun.
The shining freeways, the soft caramel
Complexes, the false fountains all come true
By forming fossils from both rose and worm
As a few impervious insects overrun
Their neighbor-species, and bore through the corm,
Continuing the damage we have done.

How obvious. How pitiful. The blurred
Stream is sterile, and mute the ragged bird,
And, worn to traces by the emptying swarm,
All but out of touch the living world.

WALTZING MATILDA

For D. and A.

One follows the small figures
Out and in, upright in the dance,
Hand painted fast to hand in the bandbox
Gazebo where they waltz with an increasing
Languor, the niceness of the curve

Of each return outdrawn
As if making an allusion
To former sweetness,
Glowing polka or gavotte.

Now the sad little tune slows down
And one looks hard into the other's face
As if about to seize
The moment when their feet
Shall bring them to stillstanding
To breathe a love as fresh as Cumberland
In adjectives like petals
About to loosen from the rose

Yet ripe with an idea the last note
Emerging with its frail
Rubato out of the run down spring
(Part of some self-conscious lyric
Life will not start again)
Quells with the long-since-ceasing
Ringing of a village bell, God's
Disappearing clangor like a stiff

Clack that wrinkles the air
In its wake, jagged as the flock
Of jackdaws darkening the square
With its market scaffolds,
The worshippers slipping off

To the Antipodes—the sky! the bush!
Quaint bandbox on the stubbly green,
Music soft with the toot of horns
In the brazen distance, pleasure
Pledged and taken, hand in hand, until

As if abashed by paradox
They all fall mute, the wind
Taken out of them, the dance
Fled on the sandy wind
That coils to the sky, all
The pretty steps like writing only
The limbs can do, only they forget.

MARBLE BABY: *Verses at Christmas*

> *"Why are they crying?"*
> *"It's the babby, sir."*
> *"Why are its arms bare?"*
> *"The babby's chilled to the marrow, sir; its clothes are frozen and do not warm it."*
> *"Why is the babby poor? Why is the steppe so bare? Why don't they embrace and kiss? Why are they so black with black misfortune? Why don't they feed the babby?"*
> THE BROTHERS KARAMAZOV, III.ix.8.

The marble baby in the nightmare stirs,
Its eyes masked under some gray clinic bandage;
Arms that seem to curve, except like rakes
They end in the blank fingers no one touches
Although stiffened piteous in need.

The dreamer bristles all along the flesh,
Sifting interpretations that throughout
These tableaux hesitate of one's decay
A tentative indictment, subtly keyed
To the pale being someone has abandoned:

The hips shrink down from the small puffy belly.
The jutting navel pulses. . . . These must tell
How haunted is the urge to help another
When not quite carried through. As if to feed,
The arms crook back and forth but they obtain

Scant nourishment from one whose only spurs
Are appetite, speed, theatre, and clamor,
Need abruptly gratified and stammered
Vows of loyalty. When one leg takes
A rough stab at the air to climb a little

(It knows not whither), plucking at the heap
Of threads of clothing in which it has lain
As in a manger no one comes to honor,
It is as if these acts plucked at the pain
That bores into its frame till it cannot sleep

Or warm its body, in the loosened wrapper
Rattled by the hand of misery
In a brutal moment—something giving way
That once subdued the impulse to be cruel
Imbedded in the violent debris

Tumbling through a spiritless universe
—Tremendous evil in the vein of clay
One treads down, casual, in daily passage.
And the sound of weeping comes, all hollowed out,
Like a bamboo clapper in a wooden bell.

*   *   *

The wailing that is heard surrounds the figure
Central as the Christchild in the *crèche*,
But it is not the marble baby crying.
It is the dream, from every hollow hope
And weakness ruining the bland dead soul

Of this low dreamer and immoderate
Pealing and ringing out to celebrate
All fascinated pity and remorse
Until, impulsively elated, hope
And shame and tasteless culpability

Wetly weep for their excessive course.

*   *   *

Blackened with black misfortune, sentinel
Who cannot warn, bell that cannot toll,
Heart that lets seep forth its warming blood,
The babby stands for, tonelessly, the good.

"Can you see to help me?" it sings out
—The little marble effigy of sheer
Forsakenness letting fall a tear
That shimmers with the faces that observe it
Crying, "Something is hurting me somewhere."

*   *   *

It must feel their presence in the snow
—Long-lashed, heraldic, the swift iron deer
Of conscience who laconically console
With steaming nostrils and slim gait the seed
Of virtue in its desolate reverse,

A forest of negation. As they near
The whimpering babby stung as if by burrs
Invisible to aiding, in the vein
And bone deep-sunken, deeper than any fear,
The thousand branches at once start to thresh

Their crystalline chaff, starring the air with grain
And haulms of ice that settle down and bead
On the dark antlers of the deer who nurse
The human child with their warm bulk and breed,
Its wan neglected body to refresh.

*   *   *

Although nothing changes—still the trivial mesh
Beneath these vivid ciphers of reprieve
Twists in the blood and chemicals foretell
What is possible—yet the dark skies uprear
These blazings it is poignant to believe:

The dreamer feels the reindeer intercede,
The suffering of the infant then abate,
The tears of all things springing at their source,
One's own heart scored through with the doubled weight
Of the wet bandages that chill the child.

One stag taps with a homing blow then breaks
Up from the breathing herd who leap to follow,
Clattering on the steppe. The small birds cheep
Gaily when the ribboned branches sway.
The poor baby wakes. And it is Christmas Day.

STOVE SICKNESS

There's a queer creaking inside me.
HANS CHRISTIAN ANDERSEN, *The Snow Man*

The leaves on the apple tree still mimicked dark
Green summer, but they snapped with nervous dread
Like leather spanned out on a sleigh and not
The living leaf. From his low mound, trodden
By children who just that day about a rake
Had pressed him up to this judgmental height,
The snow man saw that on their undersides
Snow had formed to the leaves, like padded hands.
Something like pity for these dragged-down things
Stopped him a moment.
Wind raised his outer crystals like a fur
As, not unkind, he saw how haplessly
The baleful crow cawed, and the squirrel leaped,
The rabbit sank into her tracks, the perch
Nosed beneath the deepening rind of ice
That would soon press him in his frozen bed
—But he tightened his demeanor when he found
Each source of pity stupid and abrasive
Until the abrasive seemed what he required,
Compacting him more splendidly in substance.
The beaming of the sun—how weak it was,
Flaring incompetently between
Alarming banks of cloud as if a lamp
Were being handled in a gale. Except
For the excellent cold, in fact, on him the world
Rang clumsy and offkilter and ill-keyed.
The hardy winter birds pipped joyfully
As if they could not tell their future food
Would be all hardship, while the frost around
Drove at a spanking clip, tearing along the bark's
Twisted corrugations so the seams
Blanched, and also moulding to his trunk

The snow man's head more strongly, till he blazed.
When a young skater and her beau broke past
And clapped the crusts of the wind-roughened snow
With their large feet, and their laughter shrilled like bells
Of two pitches, and the watchdog coughed
Violently after them, the snow man's
Few coarse solitary thoughts froze
Deeper with delight so that the teeth
Of the very rake crackled in his mouth.

Then he turned his wit upon the house
Closed hopefully against him. In the attic
Swinging on a rope of its own hair
A dirty onion grown too dry to eat
Hung back in the shadow like a face
Horrified at its unhappiness,
While from their parlors garishly real faces
Mowed and delved as if obedient
In emphasis to some mute gardener
Working an arid plot. The snow man groaned
His pleasure at their elbowing whose servants,
Bonneted among long silver trays,
Moved like flowers on ice—though none of these
Meant anything to him.
                                    But down in the cellar,
On its four iron legs, stood an old stove
That looked like something tethered in the corner.
He did not recognize it, yet he saw,
In its forge scars, its floral brands, its soot,
The working features of a memory
Licked at by weather from a former world.

Uneasily, the snow man stared, the day
Waned, sharply the tin goose on the gable
Turned true north, the sun's wick sputtered, but
These did not cheer him up in the old way.

Dusk at length breathed out a kind of smoke
That sullied everything with its loose film
Except the onion's writhing luminescence
(Which troubled him like an all-knowing eye)
And the square gleaming in the oven's side
Behind which moved (the snow man knew) her heart,
For when a hand cast fuel on the embers
Foaming with life, a flame shot out and flickered
On the ice ferns twined against the window
To a forest that forced him to cower
At its fire.
                    The true forest of the night
Tearing the sky in points fell soft and pat
Upon his sense, the avenue's blue ice,
The back lane's wheelruts, the closed field,
Could not draw out his shortened point of view,
While the stony moonlight seemed as poor as stone
Next to the waning orb up in the attic
And the ambling curve of the open metal thighs.
For from the warm bulge of the creature's belly
Something stirred him, harder than the cold,
As if the cold were loosening its coil
That he might stray where it was sweet but wrong
To dream he might strike through the glassy winter
—Words bolted from place: He meant strike through the window
—And go and nestle down against her, like a dog.
He wished, reflecting on, and in, the stove's light,
To quench the long pink flush that lapped so over
His face, his chest, in that red-golden cauldron
Behind the thickened plate where leaped a light
More fierce, more secret than the two pale planets'
That swam above him, one after the other
Leering, sun after moon, until his heart turned back, and halted.

Thus in the terrible blunt frost and mounting ice
He took no more delight. *I feel I'm breaking up,*

He said; *I cannot bear how pretty she is*
When she puts out her tongue. He seemed, at last,
To have forgotten even those details
That once most thrilled him with their evidence
Of winter's masterful and angry waste,
Flaring the cells of ice in his sharp hide.

Not until the weather thawed and wasted
The snow man into mist, was his lot clear:
Stove sickness struck him, and he died of it.
It was the watchdog, with forensic skill
Turning the atmosphere about the mound
Where something like a broom or hoe stood up,
Who reasoned: How injustice is undone
By time—viz., how the megalith of water
Splintered, how the torrent caught in crystal
Loosened on the stove rake in his body,
How the wave erected upon zero
(Which was the snow from which the man arose)
Eroded on the instant out of longing.
He put his head on his paws and thought it through:
To this rake, the burning oak and fardels
In the stove had called for stoking. Like had yearned
Toward like. The charring logs had hummed
And the rod of wood—his skeleton—resounded,
Pealing his substance down into a pool,
As, to the toothed iron in his rigid jaw,
The oven's lode had whispered out her sentence,
We are of one body, and must burn.

Now there was nothing left of master winter,
Only the green of a snowdrop thrust from earth
Beneath the mortal breathing of the dog.

DWELLER IN THE FOREST

This is no natural realm. Only one creature has been taken in.
Dulled, as if by smoke, the uniform firs ambiguously muster, harder
To see than early illness. Dun-gold-green pines have grown
So close, the needles have dried out on the lowest branches,
Break, and drift to the muffled floor where only crickets move.
There seems no way in. At the task of leaving, only revulsion.

Yet when I saw it, the forest was shimmering with dew and gum,
Branches profuse with curiosity that kept the outline of each leaf
Dark and clean, like a symbol. Then the trees began to sound the songs
Of each oracle—mulberry and laurel, blazing thorn, the German
        hardwoods,
Apple drenched with fruit and borne down in reverence along that
        wave . . .
Boles from which the sap sighed out when touched, pluckings
That drew forth an ichor of melancholy flowing clearly
Down the rivery bark, spirits that burned like wicks in oil
Throughout the dusk, all gave out their being with a kind of calm
To which the forest assented in a long breath of desire.

Far to the interior, past linden and oak (the conjugal pair
Roped with morning-glory), it was known lay the hole the devil used.
But nowhere myself. As if I were the traveller who had come
At some time and at some other, outworn with waiting, could go away.

MANNIKIN

From the wet starlight of the glade
A hut sends out its chink of fire.
RANDALL JARRELL

Behind that window casting its melony light
Out into the evening blue, there is no
Family basking by the fire of their future,
Which feeds itself on brownish paper money,
No son awake before the small paint jars
Fuming with resins like hot bowls of food
From which mace, cuisse, and chess-square tunic draw
Their blazing, nor a mother on a whim
Looking through the box of children's things
To see once more if she can find the corn
Of barley from which the children grew.

Nor, when you come close enough to see
What the rough-woven curtains are made of,
Do you encounter what you feared you might:
One of those loathsome confederations
Of misshapen ones making the mannikin,
Eerily lifelike, down to the third finger's
Writing callus and the faintest scars,
Obtained in childhood, echoed on the doll
Just where they still float in the flesh
Of your knee and side. (The icon's mouth would also
Whiten in an expression tearless and firm.)

Not even these sooty demons whose language is
Obscure (though, clearly, that distorted grunting
Or lapping rustle is expressive of
Delight in choosing you for this bewitchment
Which now they will begin to formalize
On the hand and face, the skin touched randomly
And with unerring harm),—not even they

55

Await you behind the glowing window in the woods.
No, the shock is that *no* coalburners
With a crookbacked grudge against your house
Are chewing roots around a grate of flames
Whose light, leaping uncannily up and down,
Limes the blowing switches of the shrubs
With a doubled flickering, like a stereopticon's.
The world no longer has much interest in
Tormenting you. The window in the woods
Is not the sign of life in the old sense,
Not even of malevolence.
Merely another nightmare image of the self
Dreaming about the speechless thing
—The world bereft of it.

*   *   *

Even as the harrowers of memory
Weaken, their old, black clothing ghostlike
Against the floorboards that take back their grain,
You sense the drift of these gross metaphors
Toward what is worse than plain. Past the window,
That spirit more familiar than yourself,
Since more observed, gathers out of the dusk
A shape that *is* his, though inaccurate
Like a twin's, his face unscored by trouble,
Younger-looking, less severe, well-built,
With a pleasant curve to his mouth as he writes at a table.
Habits have been sorted differently,
Some vestigial. Now he smokes a pipe,
Looks robust, has strangely darkened skin
(How odd, a tan). His children are
Upstairs asleep (the vision on this point
Is definite); obviously a woman made
Those curtains. He himself—a fine little man
Going about the doing of good in the world,

His strong points travestied by limitations—
Has yet suffered nothing to surprise him.

The dream upraises like a glowing wafer
This form of innocence life has destroyed
With your collusion. But the scars are healed
By never having happened, rolled up backwards
Like a silent movie though the characters
Keep ageing buoyantly, past recall. That is the sorrow
That punishes, like the pathway of the pin
Finding the midpoint of the hypnotized stare
Where all their distant happiness crowds in.

L'ESTATE

I

Black and white, the flocks of tiny creatures
Steer their feathered bodies for brief stretches
From one mock orange to another, or,
Loose on the ground, lift into the branches
Of a spruce as if melted upwards
From the earth.
                   The lines in which they fly
Weave a weft across the warp of needle
And foliage the heat will soon make dormant.

At intervals, one of these blessed, blessing,
And preoccupied bright beings (a chickadee
Or yellow-throated finch or oddly 'vertical'
Dwarf woodpecker with flecks of bleeding scarlet)
Will wholly disappear from the design

And the shuttle of their fellows carry forward

Fewer threads to the far edge of the frame,

As if long runs had been pulled in light silk.

Looking back, can you see what disappeared
From the pale work on the imaginary loom?—
The movement of sparks among the shadows, then
Ah! the deeper bands of shade against
The already quiet core of inner boughs?

I I

Clasped by the leaves, the warm birds
Hop and warble in their moment's cage
(As in Plato's apt image of random
Collations which the mind cannot
Possess). And whether what inspired them
To halt here were nothing but
A twist in the bark resembling a bronze
Beetle, or a morsel of light disguised
As a moth—would not this, too,
Shadow a mind turned hasty
By its greed? But their credulity seems
Curiously
              virtuous for these myriad birds
Are emissaries from places beyond this,
Who have taken up their bodies
Only in hypothesis. Their flamelike forms
Are, truly, burning lines
Of spirit in the tall crystalline veil
That folds incessant and mysterious across
The hedges and hummocks
Of the suspiring garden.

Obedient to symmetry, the vivid
Seams their flights draw forth
Tug to shape the summer atmosphere's
Clear skein—that seeming medium
Made of breezes, gauzy moisture,
And barely tinted panels of illumination
Curved out and rising as the whole strains
Against the long guy ropes
Like a great translucent pleasure balloon.

III

Indeed, the entire season is made almost festive by the sweet company, trim formations, and mild orderly twittering of these miniature animals—also by their fine contrastive markings with a smudge of yellow or red like an ornament on brow or throat as they flicker in the drab hard beds where the daylilies have let down their dead petals about the erect puckered seed pods.

Above all, the tiny birds cause joy by their perfect suitability to this time, in which they flourish as if the great moment in their zoological necessity coincided with the very time when men and flocks are faint, as Vivaldi wrote of deep summer, and the pine-tree burns, and one walks, sleepless and jittery at the heat lightning, through the drone of the locust and the clouds of nipping ephemerids.

IV

For the true song
birds who poured
down the sides of June
cascades of love
melodious,
          sadly
have ceased. One
sees them still:
flamboyant
cardinal drawing
off our interest from
his assiduous
dun mate (for she
tells his future),
the robin with his
rusty bib and ill
tempered gaze,
a speckled
bird with a monotonous
monopolizing
cry like a pump
handle in the prairie,
and the black foragers
who may never
have extruded any
sound who still fan
out avidly out
of order
mowing through time
with beaks
like kernels of corn.

To tempers worn
with the static siege

of heat this
last species strikes
a note almost
deliberately
stupefied, the very
      excess
of their application
become economy further
to fuel them in
the old blundering.
              How
different from those dashing
conjugal red
birds who bemusedly
comb the marigolds
for food and the pompous
pausing
robin who listens
for the worm.

V

But different from them all is the ancient
Cackling purple-wingèd crow,
Omen of insatiability
Whose numbers, fattened on the fierce mid-day,
Cruise the alleys, fight the squirrel for cob,
Tinfoil, and pulley-bone; fanatic guardians
Of offspring (now full-fledged) whose inept wails
Drench the air until the mind recoils.

The crows join in with calibrated screeches,
Drag their huge loose shadows on ball bearings
Over the innocent world, glinting like aircraft
Above the rubble they have just created:
The cities burned flat and pale, the ground baked gray
Like paving, the people hazy as vapor, and
The garden shrunk from the light back into mould.

VI

In the middle of the night,
Like thoughts too faint for daylight,
Apples, now, and again,
Fall to the cracked ground.

The comically sharp
Thudding in late summer's
Hollow is enough to
Tremble memories
Awake into the hours
When the mind without
A hope of comfort, thirsts.

Then, as the dark thins out
And the many small birds rise
Discoursing against evil,
The ravens shriek themselves
Aloft
      to their unchanged
Unanswerable manoeuvres.

August 1985

Autumn Eros

Dass auf deiner wange
Nicht der duft verwehe ...

SOUND WAVES

I *(At fourteen weeks)*

In the first negative, a shape presages
The almost human profile of the skull
Against a bolster the technician gauges
Could be placenta. Like a general
Reposed in state—or like a fogbound hull—
The infant drifts among its dim debris
Of nourishment and rigging, a vehicle
Tethered to darkness by one spectral knee,
    Rib and feature faint in quality.

II *(At sixteen weeks)*

A fortnight later, hurtling through its stages
So fast the brow has doubled, the huge null
Of the eye socket—now twice as deep—engages
The parents' with its primal monocle
(The other eye blurred by some obstacle),
As if to caution us, or disagree.
What have we done? This enigmatical
Creature has spied our mediocrity,
    Rib and feature white with gravity.

III *(At twenty-one weeks)*

Seeming to speak, a fresh image assuages
That baleful hollow glare: A chronicle
Of kind floats forth and riffles through the pages
Of its movements. After an interval
With an arm upraised, to mark the body's lull,
Something like smiling flickers on the screen,

In recognition of its own sweet will
Buoyed above the molten vertebrae,
    Rib and feature warm with clemency.

Envoi

A second view looks from the fontanelle
Down through the shining oval cavity
Where thread is spun. The spine curves in this well
Like a rope dropped from the vertex to that sea
    Where rib and feature weave their history.

While in the last one, and most personal,
The feet we know as hers lie sleepily
Side by side, but not quite parallel.
Each is bird-like, or like a fluted shell,
Yet close to home, just as her self would be,
    And ribbed and featured with humanity.

ANGEL FOOD

Thought is made fruitful by love.
GONCHAROV, *Oblomov*

Unnaturally dark today,
   The streetlights have come on.
      Above our daughter's cradle
(Ribbed and round, its keel
   Rolling down the whitecaps of her sleep
      Shipped by her hungry dream)
There twist on lines of air
   The three woolen angels banded
      From brow to throat to waist
—Like warriors of light—
   By haloes of minutely scalloped gold
      Silk wire, at last loosening
In the long thin sashes
   That glint in their foaming robes.

      They float at their three heights like three
Ideas of Beauty, Truth, the Good
   Touching the central hub
      From which they fall—a corolla
Of twigs with a visionary burnish—
   Before they touch each other.
                           Rather
      Their wings float through their sisters'
Like ragged sun-flocked clouds,
   Beauty wafted by the gown of Good, Goodness
      Slow beneath the combings of the True—
But touched to transmutation
   No less thoroughly for lightness
      As by the open rainbow of a prism
(Itself too icy hard to tear).
   And if like the moods and virtues
      The angels' bodies mesh with the thin air,

They make the abstract fruitful by their love
    For underneath the hem the legs are *there*,
        Winnowing the laden atmosphere.

So I have watched,
    Through the doorway to her room
        At the end of this brief
Louring afternoon,
    Body dissolved in mind:
        The angel mobile swayed
By the odd draft against a sky
    That suddenly blossomed
        With heavily shaken snow,
Causing the hedge to stutter and the knotty
    Trunk of fir to stand dark
        Upright in its sheath of white-
Fringed air, and I saw how everything
    Whitened, warmed, rose
        Higher to the sight as if the mind
Had broken from its hood
    Or skimmed off several hoods in ever paler
        Translucencies like spangled
Panes until it saw without
    The medium of brooding,
        And relished everything
Dancing and cold, while almost shyly
    The little yards themselves
        Shook off old pocks and rubble,
Smoothed exquisitely into custards
    Beneath the sugared trees
        And sprinkled fans of evergreen,
The soft fast snow impersonating
    Infant joy, in a caprice
        Making its angel food
Out of the very stuff of angels,
    Lightness, joie de vivre, love

Of all that is fair, and just,
Fair and pleasing and blessèd and breathless and just,
On which the mobile's angels look
Faintly stirred by sympathy,
Leaning a little back so they might
Cast aloft their countenances.

Now when the baby wakes with a blind cry
I hold her up to the pale angelic shapes
Whom she fixes with her eyes
As her new body
Settles and glows
And we seem both uplifted
Glistening with heat
Against the dusk-blued snow.

When I lay in the hospital
Waiting for this child
To be coaxed forth, I thought of heaven
As a closet where she hung
Looking down on me month
Upon month, until it seemed
To smother her
I knew so little.
Medicine kept trying to acquaint us
On the surface and again offered up
Her heartbeat on the monitor
goodbye goodbye goodbye
—I heard this, fearless.
I watched the liquid
Dropping from the tube into one arm
(A "vitamin," said the waggish nurse)
But as yet felt nothing.
At night unhooked
So I could "rest," I lay listening

To the woman in the next bed, diabetic,
    Black, her belly big
        As a drum, a slave
To freakish sugar levels,
    The baby's heavy drowse,
        And the machines that scolded her.
The sonar plaque strapped
    Above the fetus quivered
        As her bulk quivered in receipt
Of the worst TV I had ever overheard,
    Reruns and comedies till morning,
        Servile with false hilarity.
Sending out the hot aroma
    Of vanilla in rising yellow cake
        As if a saint were passing,
The big girl laughed (or moaned)
    And the baby's heartbeat worked free
        Of its sensor, plunged into
A wilderness of static
    As into expanding
        Darkness where nothing recurred,
Every beat uniquely weak,
    Sent out but never answered.
        (How can one acquiesce
Even in neutral
    To the loss of the beloved?)
        Then, the mattress giving, the machine
Picked up again the inner voice
    With the sound, at first, of glass
        Ticked by rain, then of metal, heating,
Then, more furious, of a gallop
    Of hooves tingling on cracked clay
        And a real rough rider out of a true
Rerun *ka-thung ka-thung ka-thung*
    —Leather gulping as the hero whipped
        His pony toward foothills like unshaven cheeks

Whose whiskery flags crackled
   In a wind like baking soda
      And her baby was back in range.

Every room along the problem ward
   Sent forth at night these worn-out rhythms,
      Comically shabby—flickering signals,
Fatuous dialogue, and barks of music
   Cut with the throbbing of goodbyes (*goodbye*
      goodbye) with random gaps in the measure
Like station breaks, scurrying empty patches
   To which nobody jumped—echoes of both
      Mothers' and their creatures' hearts,
Twinned machineries of need
   Sad and ordinary,
      Bulky with long passivity.

My child was being drawn ("induced")
   Down into all this tube and tracery
      Network of spectral nourishments,
Body and mind dissolved in a second sense
   So neither grew, set on each other
      Like dogs snarling with hunger
But too cumbersome to spring.
   That was the impression: Extreme
      Liveliness, eyes snapping with light
In a kind of mania,
   But on a skeleton exaggerated
      Like knobby coral
And sedimented with florets of fat
   Till I was anxious lest the very molecules
      Of modern matter and image and air
Ruin the child into age,
   Hasten her clock, induce
      Consciousness before memory to the point
Of lethargy from the American emptiness,

The great contradictory emptiness
    That made life far too gross to lift.

But then I saw, falling through my heart,
    My fear for her as fear of her—
        More, as the wish to shrink back
To the form we had before the seed was lodged.
    Could we not lift up, hovering, lightly
        Crumble into a fine dust,
And then ride off in a little wind?

This was why I lay
    On my left side willing myself
        To contemplate abstractly
Abstract filaments of thought,
    Goodness, Truth, Beauty,
        Sainthood, bereavement,
Stalemate and habit,
    Fair limbs in daylight,
        Uncomplaining, in my way invisible,
Airy-infinite, like Blake's Albion
    Drowsing above the salvageable world in the pale
        Limbs of his eternal individuality,
All his children from his bosom
    Fleeing away, wandering outside
        Of humanity,
            so big and faded, like him,
So willing to muse and tolerate
    Till things let go,
        I hoped to be forgotten.

But the little girl was already matter
    And she did not forget.
        The third day of prompting
Brought me into focus,
    Then my flesh began to rain,

And on through another night and day
The torrents crossed
   As I labored to be as little
      In the way of the quakes of separation
As they themselves would let me be,
   Until at dreadful length out
      In the air, breathing
What the planet provided, she
   Took to it as well, she shone
      In it, with it she wept. Thin air
Belled out the ribcage
   Smaller than my palm and made
      A voice miniature yet fiery
Like the lid of her eye rounded by red-gold lashes,
   The line of her mouth conformed
      To its first samplings of the dry
Expanses, tasting
   —And being—the bread of a new life.

Now I can hold her while she eats,
   All fretfulness dissolved
      In pleasure, can feast on her
In a world that runs,
   That rains with life.
      The snow swings
Crossways in sheets,
   Silky manes that jump up, and shiver,
      Jubilant at something, a little
Unmanageable, while the angels
   Drift in their dome
      Of suggestion, thinking to themselves:

Angel Food

> Beauty, Truth, the Good
> Blessèd to shape oneself
> After them, in mind
> Some craving of the fact
> For the form, some following
> By decent deed of the fit desire
> And idea of grace: Fairness
> Reclined on stillness
> Facing heavenward,
> Whence the manna comes.

(December–January   1985–1986)

THE CURRENT

Midnight and thereafter. I keep stirring her awake.
I know. I could defer to the tidal pull of sleep
Almost too great for me to surface against,
Which will replenish, against my will, my will.
But I still shrink before the actions of release:
My dry back bending, hand curved underneath her heart,
The cradle rocking against my unsteady cold thigh
As if I were placing her for burial in an open boat
Pushed out upon the combers steep with moon-rime
Where the future rides in the ebb of shadow where I am not,
Feeding its featureless child, the harm of mine.

Yet once she is released, it is as if her body,
Unworked upon, unthreatened, instantly gave itself
Over to another life, diluted, elemental,
As, when one leans down to the golden infusion
Of the lake to loose them there, a dozen minnows
A while hold up the round shape of the sieve
From the bait bucket and weave above it like the fumes
In a reagent jar. But flexing in the water's porousness
Until the walls to whose solution they still sluggishly
Adhere sheer to carved currents of emptiness
In the deep,
                one by one they dart wild.

Stalled, soon, in flight, the fishes, at a signal
Pausing near the twilit masses of deflected light
Grazing the strange mirrory flanks and indistinct clamp
And creak of a heavy mouth, they scare themselves together,
Recall the forgotten fish-shape of the school—mute oval
Collecting like a pupil in the great dimming bowl
That uses them to read the staccato script of tears
Of ink, which is all they are: The cheapest bait

Swimming the long tense cluster, like a slatted cage,
Across the few leagues of their freedom.

So as I let her down the baby's torso drifts into suspension,
Subsiding to a fresh pattern. Her breathing turns down and in
One degree, banked by a distant drawing off of the current
To fade her from me, veining blue the membrane over her eye,
Mouth parting on a thread of blackness as her hand holds
Tight to the cloth she brings across her face, on which the fish
Will curve like legends through the sparse preconscious night.

ZODIAC

This one of her asleep, her lids light blue
Across the wells of consciousness—her breath
Half halting made ours almost falter too,
Italicizing our near nothingness,
age hair ash skin
                    lapped by her complex nearness.

Here she is looking at a leaf
Among a sea of them the frost turned brown.
What does she see from that decaying reef?
Why will she not stop looking down?

The more we yearn toward her as she sleeps,
Riffling through absences,
The more unlike her, face by face, these seem

And the more the changeable world turns cold and slow,
Expression blanker as we lose the drift.

Torment of tree in stasis the hiss of snow,
With its flailing, filters through, muttering loss
To them that have ears—all this tomorrow will show
Huge and amusing. But tonight it frightens us.

Until, when the light is out, laid on her bed
For all the winter like a thing of fur,
Along her torso as I tend to her
The figures of the stars stand out like amber.

In this eccentric lighting I see her head
Turn toward me, watchful, luminous,
As if she saw above her, in the star-spur
Static that played between us, linking us
Back to pain, nothing to make her cower.

AUTUMN EROS

When she came down, the child's composure held,
Ununderstanding she was far away
From the familiar. The glint of loud machines
So natural, like birds—these were the same,
As were we two, flared in attitudes
Fending and succorant and faintly dazed
Above her stroller with its clicking wheels
Which she leans out breathtakingly to see.
Turning in the airy element
Triumphant, like a porpoise in its hoop,
To look back up at us, her torso long,
Her finger pointing up to where she marks
Our recognized, reflecting consciousnesses,
She shows her pleasure in the pleasure she commands
From everything, her very hands amused
At their adroitness and obedience.
And our breath is caught, as it was not in flight.

It is as if she burned the atmosphere.
Like heat wicked from a star, or the gold ions
Poured down from an angel's mouth and forehead,
The look of flame licking her upturned face
Licks at us, too.
                    But in our flush of awe
Is something half-done, doubted, and withheld
While she is all ignition, full, by turns,
And hungry and then fed—a kindling cosmos
Avid in combustion and in speed
Ideal to extremes, as if her mind,
The same now as it was, were . . . not at ease.
She helps disturb her own amenities
Till every posture is uncomfortable
Bearably, precarious containment
That displays what she can almost do
As she heals toward the stamina of strain

In whose shade she will see through what she knows
Into the unforming dusk of action.

We hardly notice these, complexities
She lives with for a moment over months
As each new stage is trod and broken through.
Still, her little urgencies of mood
Rise up and pour down us like sheer time,
That pool of rippling vistas, pastel, free,
Mist-barred, element in which we breathe
Till quietly drunk with her, our tiny Eros.
Once, perhaps, we felt so for each other:
That we were the secret the other one was keeping,
Even the air the other one was breathing
In rhythm with the rain that bathed the planet,
The food the other one drank in by gazing
So if that gaze extinguished, we should die,—
As, in a way, we have. Simply died out
In our embering honeycomb of coal.
Now she is the flame-wrapped secret. The first
Thing in the mind on waking. Warm contagion
Of awareness and delight. A draught
Of what in us, long since, was the elixir.
One taste of this brings all the losses back.

Old enough to be grandparents, we
Are met by her grandparents at the gate.
They, too, have had their losses, seeing by stages
Coarsen all their tender potencies
And all the gleanings taken from their hands.
They have waited for us during the bland summer
Into which they fall each day, grown smaller
In those husks, bright-eyed, less reachable,
And fainter yet the little heat of August.
Why did we wait so long? I ask their faces
Crinkled with relief. I ask their old eyes.

Connections hard to make, we travel far
To reach them in their Northern solitude
Thronging with dread news from the clear broadcasts
Brought down by a costly huge antenna.
We bring them, almost speechless for our part,
Stunned into postures by unhappiness,
A late new life, brimming up with meaning
But blurred against the syllables that tumble
Wisely torrential from the half-heard console,
The medium delirious with words
To which they hardly listen, as if the vast
Emergencies that loom up on the screen
At home, the dire thump and drumming on the road,
Were laboring in their bloodstream now, disarming
Them for what (amid the habits of
Their distance, their fond weaknesses—his temper,
Tolerated, her drowse of mind, also,
Amid small virtues clung to out of love)
Broaches the future through a tiny hole.
Alone, together, under everything, they hear it
Like a dropped pin, their eyes darkened and wide,
Their whole being riveted elsewhere
Like the reclining dog, hair stiffened at
A signal one cannot take her staring from
So if one touches her, she feels like wood:
Something comes to them from out of the cold,
Which, even in summer, whistles the topmost leaves,
Touching on news of the worst snow yet that gathers
Force from all their wasted time beneath
Whose drifts, this year or next, they would lie down.

How much more clear the rivery addresses
Of the baby, her repertoire of features
Not quite placeable, fresh expression
Fleeting across her face like a high swallow
Threading above unmapped, fog-roughened country,

A no-man's land of bracken and burnt pine
Like the one we drive through now, strung with marinas,
Bait-and-tackle stores, and novelty bars,
For which, I am glad, she lacks the analogues,
But not the interest: Cars are *heavenly*!
Next best to being in one, scenes ticking past
(She excels my father in absorption
In the literal eloquence of tools),
Is seeing them pour down the road like playthings,
Tiny motors throbbing, then extinguished,
Headlamps touching the earlier darkening air
Among the elusive signals of the fireflies
Which she can't focus yet, they are so brief.

How automatically we turn to her
Interests as a way to cancel ours,
A welcome emptying of everything,
We think, until a moment's thought returns
All other obligations to her cause,
Making of me, their firstborn, and my firstborn,
Of me and mine, and them, a sort of triptych
Whose darkened figures hover in a mute
Numinous void as on a gilded icon
Which haunts us, now it has no power to heal.

Time and again I reach this point of darkness
Without a complementary span of light.
But the days do pass in a recuperative
Lull, good for the lungs but rather sad
And for the women a great deal of work
While broken nerves consign you to the shadows.
Dad in the garage toys with a broken
Tape recorder under a harsh light
Like a watchmaker's while the reel spins
Helplessly quiet. Geese like inky letters
Stumble across the sky in noisy flight.

Each patch of woods has one tree that has turned
Translucent like a candle set in daylight.
The water in the lakes is now too cold to swim.

Evenings, the four of us sit down to poker,
Elated by the fading hour and season
So mildly, it seems personal and random.
I have said less than ever to my parents
And they to me.
The woodstove hums, filling the air with fine
Thin smoke, someone forever opening the door
So we can breathe, but then we get too cold
And we jump up to push it shut again—
A little game with a little law of life
That says it is never perfect at the moment.
But for the moment something has been stanched
In the gash of time. My mother's hands
Get no more gnarled in this half-hour nor do her hopes
For moderation in my father's habits
Anxiously flicker. She is lovely. Calm
Treads out the dark hairs on my father's hand.
He bets too much—to throttle things to life
So all the drab recessive moods and secrets
Mooning about him with mysterious rhythm
Would leap up orderly to seek his grasp.
You smile at me. We play the cards we are dealt.
One door away, the baby falls asleep
Moaning a two-note thing that soon is one.

CIRCADIAN

How dark the day is
But not with the plummeting
That freshens the heart.

*　*　*

Rain so long falling,
Drops emerge upon a wire
Like distant starlight.

*　*　*

The humus soaking.
Plant, with the slug trailing off—
Eternal couple.

*　*　*

Apples like walnuts.
Bluejays demonically
Spoil what they disdain.

*　*　*

Quarrel remembered . . .
Slow storm, the baby asleep.
Insomniac's cheer.

*　*　*

Stuporous nighthawks
Haul through their grating pattern,
Crosshatching sky's end.

*　*　*

Like the serious
Birdclatter as the dawn comes,
The child in her dream.

*　*　*

When I lift her up
She looks down at her night world
Deliberately.

FAITH

How should I let her go?
                    Her hair in fine
Sparse waves conforms to a small glowing head.
In all lights she looks thoughtful like a smith
Gathering up his blow.
Chirps issue from her high and spirited

When the shadows pass.
                    Hi, hi, she calls,
Looking from them to me if no reply
Cascades upon her watching, then we sing
The reasons why, alas,
Few of them hear. I love her till I die.

How sad to look at her.
                    And yet, wrenching
Me out of doubt, the radiant consciousness
Of her hand patting me when we embrace,
The role of comforter
Come easy, with its healing practices.

True, I will go before,
                    a failing scene
The background to what might have been,
That life of infant calm continuing
Forever now the substance of the hoped for
And clue to any clue not touched or seen.

THIS PHOEBE

I

The child is speaking on the instrument again, a puzzle
Of blocks that clamp together in a cubist nest of forms
That feels to her like a telephone. She is calling Lynn,
Serious and friendly says *my mother* (a phrase she has never used),
Then from that miniature net of signs already clinging to her speech
She loosens the accusative, new pronoun *her*, about whom her eager
Truths burst in a long waterfall of expletive rejoinders to another,
As I lean toward her trying to catch her drift about me.

Even at home, she draws herself over to her other home—*This Phoebe,*
She announces, sure to be understood—where people talk to her
All day I think about her every gesture, and she to them, admonishing,
Excusing—telling them what we do? how we sing in the dark?
How my temper flares?—the earnest and incurable address poured out
Like the warble of winter birds in their own language describing
Seed sprinkled on the ice, where to be found, what danger,
Till, birdlike, her thoughts alight far out of range, trying the current
In her mind that would carry her back to me.

                                        When she is gone
To sleep, the scatterings of things she bears about
With her all day, exchanged from room to room, resemble
Flotsam in nests, the last scraps of cloth still warm
From where she folded them about her toys, remonstrating with
Or praising them, depending on the way the words unfolded.

I I

Between her and the world the skeins
Of longing weave and interfade,
Conform to something she might hold,
Read, read to, or be read to by,
Nature, even human nature like a scheme
She cannot decipher yet, her people
Vaporous as words trembling with sense
As if emerging from that earlier life
Where truth spoke from the air, once
Inspirited, and heavy with kind.

III

Although it is only the sunken image
Of a telephone in a book, she tries
To lift it from its lost horizon,
Raise it into life so she can say,
Tender and starry with the privilege,
This Phoebe. Look at that folk.
Each remark electrifying
In its ambiguity—seldom about the present,
Except that all time is present there,
Feathered by slight changes in refrain,
Further softened by her perfect conviction
That she is speaking in *our tongue.*

And I remember breakfast, gazing out
Through the spider border of frost
To the neighbor's car wreathed in exhaust,
Which she breathed out as *folk,*
Wonderstruck at the ways of the world,
The habit of the cold and faery
Gesture of ascent.

IV

Now, to talk is not just something
That we do, she and I, but something I
Can do without her, until she weeps
With jealousy and I cut short the call,
Tend her so the flurried shapes
Of our repose resume their plane.
I smooth out the page of broken tracks
Where she left off.
            This Phoebe
Imitates, training for distance:
Refusing to be overheard, she breaks in
Upon her urgent eloquence with someone else
To shoo me back to work. Not until I am not
Listening does she find her place,
Quiet the room into reflection
Only she may break,
Where she would rather
Be, that room beyond the obstacle
Of blocks where she waits for me
Each day, in letter as in image, drawing
Thirstily upon the hours as they well up
To body forth the tears she does not shed
Across the surface set before her.

V

Picture falls on picture on Lynn's floor
As evening falls and the child learns
At last the pool has been drawn out
By her effort, and utterly filled with light.
At her feet, the other images
Train on the one idea. Long rays
Stride down from great orbs of gold
To the errant knots of earth,
Conjuring their union until she can
Run toward the light she surely summons
To the dusk-filled door; I enter; the hours snap off
Like veering birds who have that instant caught
A glint from the shifting lozenges of large
Perplexed surface in the room where a child
Dances and weeps, her life
A throng of sense and form
Elided by anxiety.
Clinging to my legs, *This Phoebe*,
She declares to the others there, as if to fail
One moment even in her fleeting discourse of it would
Lose her the world she made: *This my*.

DRAWING THROUGH FEVER

Already warm, the cravings draw up through her
To fly out in a fever of misbehavior, spurring her
Into my arms, my lap—my permission. Once home,
They charm her wrist to hold back mine as her free hand,
With a curl of pleasure gaining the forbidden pen,
Touches the corner of the writing tablet, then a patch of words
About some earlier emanation of her being in my stirred love,
Which she prepares to seize.
                              Possession brings a lull
Of blessedness. Even her eyes stare down in bliss
And smile out sideways when she clasps the secret things
She hopes to dissolve against her hands until
She can fuse them inward to a safer place. She does not ruin
These except when thwarted of them. Then, to ruin me,
Reckless, she thrashes even the joys so slowly craved.

My knees are mottled blue from her heels, left to swing
(But coolly) in a swoon of patience against the flesh
That silently bears her up. Then what with fever more burning
Her back and thigh the more frail her frame becomes, the limit
Of her waiting faints in her, the very threshold of excess
Imperceptible—it is like treading a ray of moonlight
On the floor: Suddenly, one is through it, the glint
Across the ankles startling, like a blow. Then one almost
Leaps into unhappiness, threshed out of sleep, and thirsting. . . .

Save that, before *her* moment broke against her, she was content
For several minutes moored in my lap, both of us damp
With her illness, to color on a page already used
For a small knot of her green "touchings" of the paper
In a former style (when she pressed the crayon into the heart
Of the sheet and held it there, hushed, happy, doing the work
Of steadfastness). But see, with a fresh stony sunny blue,
She draws so gently over the page, it is as if
Her fever were drawing through her, teaching her

To deepen the close stubs of green where lines of pure
Ultramarine spider back across those darkening groves;
While drifting light, lighter, in her abstraction,
As on the poles of silver traced by Miró over emerging
Emptiness, she draws her thought above the arm's kind calm.

These images of soul may favor her in the blind jags
Of tedium and illness when the dry spell of life is on her,
Although, once she began to fret toward my work again,
I could just make her a primitive moon spangled with a few rays
Of reminiscent blue, before the page was drawn away from me.

LEARNING THE WORLD

You sad? she asks, settling into her father's chair
The blue balloon. Fussing at the package string
That tethers it, she grows distressed,
Bemusedly, with how it dips and wobbles
Its ambiguous reply, takes it in hand:
I am so angry. To say she crooned
This scolding, or scolded with her love,
Would not yet raise that empty note of awe,
As when one of us, set somehow against her,
Would rake a ragged bolt across her joy,
Crosshatch the same plateau she tore along
When, feet sparkling, head down like a colt's,
Veering, she relearned how clean a thing was will,
How true its clatter deep down in the floor,
How right the rightness of our huge annoyance—
As if this were her judgment, which pleasantly
She lays at the balloon: You make me *an*gry.

This mood of edifying ease, however—
An opportunity to lift the voice
Against, but not to break, the rule of size
That made it dangerous to shout at us—
Clouds into her urge to punish back
Within a bolder storm of fellow feeling
Tumbled upon the facing role, she tugging at
The aimless mass that had no weight—
The bad behaving thing she recognizes
Is like herself—it, too, dazed by the racket
One spirit makes another spirit make. One hand
Against her eyes, she orders it: You comfort me.

Sweetly, the blue skin gives, where she presses it—
And almost breaks with each deflecting ardor
Until she is assuaged into another
Fury of happiness it will not take

Her long to run to ground.
                              Down the hall hurrying,
The blue globe seems to bubble in her wake,
Swayed by resistance and warming to
The fluff and hair drawn like loose ciphers
Across its curve—a map of something
On whose random path these traces ravel,
Knotted as kin, narrow as the way.

CANICULA

Fireflies float noiseless
In the high, perturbing din
Of the late locust.

*   *   *

The orchard dying—
Trunks badged with disease lean down,
Tranquil in their thirst.

*   *   *

In air hard as sand,
Now the sun boils off to blue,
Moths sip from a leaf.

*   *   *

Heat-heavy creatures
Wake and feed on their diet
Of self and other.

*   *   *

Want, predation, sleep.
Often all of these at once
In nature; in dream.

*   *   *

Among mosquitoes
Their spears half clouding, blue spruce
Defend the portal.

*   *   *

Glinting like water
But incapable of touch,
Youth, its swift old strength.

*   *   *

But her arm—damp, small—
She is not part of the wheel . . .
Her pretty breathing.

TO A CHILD WITH GLASSES

As I leave you, discs of frozen tears, Dantean
Emblems, catch and slowly shed reflection
Behind the closing scrim of summer in another
Woman's house, disorderly with order,
Weeping, round-songs, games. . . .
                                    When you turn back, in time
(When I drive off), and sink among the others'
Children to work out the ills of anyone
Alongside added sorrow, the specific separation
That, to write, I heap on you, I still see
Your lenses' half-lit glinting, smoky with distance.

And was it (inarticulate, eternal) worth
This adjectival artifice, passing strand
And briefly syntax-spangled swatch of words?

Even to write this, so long thereafter, I have had—
Catching in a thought your need against my body,
My skin furry with the curve of your quiet,
My mouth filling with the kiss I cannot think where to pour
First as I find the form for this delicious in-
Decisive swarming up of love's own fountain—cool, wild—
Heavily torn between draught and brimming, drink and weeping,
Hung at one drop, one word,—I have had, it seems,
To make a few, give or take, of those attractive
Phrases, to leave you in somebody else's arms.

PHILOMEL

. . . und fremd
Erscheinen und gestorben mir
Der Seeligen Geister.
                    HÖLDERLIN

We lift our voices from the dusk beside them: Hello Phoebe;
Philomel, hello (they are almost twins). But we sound too lonely
To bring off the comradely manoeuvre. Looking back and forth
Across their lacy work of hours, subtle with humor,
They smile into each other's eyes. O shadow
With the honey tongue. . . . *This* little girl,
I remind my husband, is the one we never had;
She keeps Phoebe company. To this our child says, ya.
Unborn yet, slipped from time, that one agrees by swaying
In and out of attention like a leaf shadow.
Warm currents of merriment course against their bodies.

Together they will carry out her passages—from infancy,
From home, our stricken brooding over Phoebe and her need
To be cheered on by what we say. Already she is less
Mindful of what moves in our darkening circle. Better their
Communion should flare forth in correspondences,
Glints on water, for the inward eye, so that the world—
On which they are, insensibly, dependent—will be bemused.

*   *   *

Watch over your sister swallow, nightingale. People the sad
Spring twilights, haunted by those clouds of blue flowers,
Draw out the skein of time to come in gaiety, kind ripples
Of melody that spring high, high in the trees where the air
Has grown too cold for beast or parasite, and we have died.

But if you could, little spirits, make yourselves warm
In your cage threadbare of comforts woven about
The great thing in your keeping, the loom of repetitions,

You might find in your quieted hearts, at the radiant hour,
The knowledge of how bitter is our loss—to see the souls
Of the blessed at last, and find them fading,
And you will forgive us then that we were old.

A SOUL CAKE

> The lanes are very dirty
> My shoes are very thin
> I have a little pocket
> To put a penny in
> > *The Cheshire Souling Song*

> the night is so dark
> the way so short
> why do you not break
> o my heart
> GEOFFREY HILL, *The Pentecost Castle*

Childish words so comforting
apple penny pocket hosen salt
Why does she not offer
Solid things to me

Too light for this wind
I am smaller now
Than I have been
The child I leave
Like a strong room
Walls aglow
A swimming hive
With all my blessing
Fire gone in

Can you warm me
For a moment
Little one

*   *   *

What if I can never make her see me
What if the soft taps in sequence
Be mistaken
If I move toward her lips
Will she dance up with alarm
Flail her arms in that way
Riddling my heart
She cannot mean to shun me by it

*   *   *

Driven over the earth so weak
I cannot reach her lintel
Blown past the hearth mouth
Rounding her sleeve with warmth
I am cold the track hard with sleet
Night grown so much longer

Even in the powdery lapse of noon
Beginning to reel with lethargy
Wings thin as humming
From an ember
And as soon to cease

                    O all things
Are readying but I cannot
The distance to go so short
So terrifying I
Cannot force myself over
Give back my ghost
To this indefinite scattering
Ever further
From what I was

NOTES

Sources for the epigraphs to the three sections are as follows: The stanza introducing *Lunar Frost* appears as the last quatrain of Louise Bogan's "'Come, Sleep . . .'" (1941). The lines that open *L'Estate* are from Edwin Muir's poem "The Place of Light and Darkness" (1937). The lines on the part title page of *Autumn Eros* translate "Lest from your young cheek / The fragrance float away," from Stefan George's "*Sieh mein kind ich gehe*" (1895).

HAPPY FIELDS: This touching encounter between Adam and Dante is described in the *Paradiso* (1318–1321), canto XXVI.

ELD, lines 6 and 145–149 echo *Ecclesiastes* 9:6 ("the dead . . . have no more for ever any share in all that is done under the sun") and 3:11 ("[God] has put eternity into man's mind so that he cannot find out what God has done from the beginning to the end."); *Psalms* 139:13 is also alluded to ("For . . . thou didst knit me together in my mother's womb").

　　Lines 115–120: These lines are a free translation of lines 6 through 9 of Hugo von Hofmannsthal's "*Terzinen über Vergänglichkeit*" (1894) whose speaker is surprised "*Dass alles gleitet und vorüberrinnt/ Und dass mein eignes Ich, durch nichts gehemmt,/ Herüberglitt aus einem kleinen Kind/ Mir wie ein Hund unheimlich stumm und fremd.*"

　　Lines 155–157 recall William Wordsworth's "Ode: Intimations of Immortality from Recollections of Early Childhood" (1807), strophe 5: "The Soul that rises with us, our life's Star,/ Hath had elsewhere its setting,/ And cometh from afar."

DWELLER IN THE FOREST. This poem began in response to the philological suggestion that the word *dwell* is related to older forms of words for *dull* and *smoke*.

　　"spirits that burned like wicks in oil": See Lawrence Durrell, "On Mirrors" (1954), "A man and woman lying sun-bemused/ In a blue vineyard by the Latin sea,// Steeped in each other's minds and breathing there/ Like wicks inhaling deep in golden oil."

L'ESTATE, "Plato's apt image of random/ Collations which the mind cannot/ Possess": The aviary in the *Theaetetus*, 197.

　　"When men and flocks are faint, and the pine-tree burns": From the sonnet introducing "*L'Estate*" (Summer), one of the concerti in *Le Quattro Stagioni* (The Four Seasons), 1726, by Antonio Vivaldi.

　　This poem was composed in August 1985, near the fortieth anniversary of the bombing of Hiroshima.

ANGEL FOOD, lines 186–191, "Blake's Albion . . . in the pale limbs of his eternal individuality,/ all his children from his bosom/ fleeing away, wandering outside/ of humanity": See William Blake, *The Four Zoas/ The Tor-*

> *ments of Love and Jealousy in/* THE DEATH AND JUDGMENT/
> *of Albion* THE ANCIENT MAN (1797), I.467 and 558–559.

THIS PHOEBE: In gratitude to Lynn Kendall.

CIRCADIAN (title): lit., "about the length of a day," a term (used by both biologists and therapists) that refers to chronic physical rhythms, especially as they govern patterns of sleep and wakefulness.

FAITH: See *Hebrews* 11:1, "For faith is the substance of things hoped for, the evidence of things not seen."

> "I love her till I die": See the Jacobean ballad "There Is a Lady Sweet and Kind."

CANICULA (title): The "dog days," which fall in the hottest stretches of July and August, when the dog star (Sirius, in the constellation Canis Major) rises and sets with the sun. In the Midwest in recent years, summer droughts have been changing the ecology (also, subtly, the psychology) of the region.

PHILOMEL (epigraph): "And strange/ They appeared, and dead to me,/ The souls of the blessed" (Friedrich Hölderlin, "*Lebensalter*," 1800).

A SOUL CAKE, "The lanes are very dirty" (epigraph): *dirty* (*OED* 4) can refer to weather, meaning *foul, stormy, muddy, wet*. I suspect this word, especially as used in the "Cheshire Souling Song," of carrying as well a strong suggestion of *cold*. "Souling" is the British dialect term for the seasonal rite of begging at Christmas and on the haunted festival of All Souls'.

Mary Kinzie was born in 1944 in Montgomery, Alabama. She attended college in the Midwest then went on to study at the Free University of Berlin and Johns Hopkins. She has assembled critical books on Borges and on American little magazines as well as editing collections of contemporary poetry and fiction. Recognized for her work in poetry as well as essay by the Poetry Society of America, the Illinois Arts Council, and the MacDowell Colony, she is also the recipient of a Guggenheim Fellowship in Poetry. Mary Kinzie is the author of three earlier books of poems, *The Threshold of the Year*, winner of the 1982 Devins Award, and *Masked Women* and *Summers of Vietnam*, published together in 1990. She is currently director of the creative writing program and the Koldyke Outstanding Teaching Professor at Northwestern University.

A NOTE ON THE TYPE

The text of this book is set in Linotype Garamond No.
3. It is not a true copy of any of the designs of Claude
Garamond (1480–1561), but an adaptation of his
types, which set the European standard for two cen-
turies. It probably owes as much to the designs of Jean
Jannon, a Protestant printer working in Sedan in the
early seventeenth century, who had worked with Garamond's romans earlier, in Paris, and who was denied
their use because of the Catholic censorship. Jannon's
matrices came into the possession of the Imprimerie
Nationale, where they were thought to be by Garamond
himself, and so described when the Imprimerie revived
the type in 1900. This particular version is based on an
adaptation by Morris Fuller Benton.

Composition and printing by
Heritage Printers, Charlotte, North Carolina.
Bound by Kingsport Press, Inc.,
Kingsport, Tennessee
Designed by Harry Ford